GET THE JOB

The Ultimate Guide to Building A Winning Modern Résumé to Establish Your Brand Value and Give You an Edge Over the Competition

Dedication

This book is dedicated to everyone taking the steps to strive for more, who are not comfortable with average.

GET THE JOB: The Ultimate Guide to Building A Winning Modern Résumé to Establish Your Brand Value and Give You an Edge Over the Competition

© 2018 Career Global, LLC

All rights reserved. No part of this book shall be reproduced, stored in a retrieval system, or transmitted by any means - electronic, mechanical, photocopying, recording, or otherwise - without written permission from the author.

The information in this book is distributed on an "as is" basis without warranty. Although every precaution has been taken in the preparation of this book, the author assumes no responsibility for any liability assumed for damages resulting from the use of the information contained herein.

Table of Contents

My Career Story	6
Document Strategy	7
Mastering Grammar	9
Résumé Styles	13
Design, Style, and Typeface	15
Gathering Information	18
Building Your Résumé	20
The ATS-Friendly Résumé	30
Cover Letters: Brief and Bold	31
The Future of Résumés	32
Putting It All Together	33
Post-Résumé Brand Strategy	47
Common FAQs	49
Samples	52
Bonus	60

Author's Note

My grandmother always said that I should have been born a rich man's daughter. I've always had big dreams, dreams too big that required too much money and were deemed unrealistic. I always figured that things would fall into place because I had a plan.

Being young and ambitious caused me to do stupid things like take nine hundred dollars and head to Los Angeles, dreaming of success but returning home two weeks later, broke. Or, buying a one-way bus ticket to an audition with no way of getting home thinking, "I'll cross that bridge when I come to it."

Even after my plans didn't work out, I'd just make more. Nothing worked until I surrendered to God's plan and relied on Him to reveal my purpose. I'm stubborn, and as "Ms. Independent," I can be determined to do it my way, regardless of the complications. I'm blessed that through it all, He gives me plenty of chances to get it right.

Because of my Lord and Savior Jesus Christ's grace, mercy, sacrifice, and unwavering love, I'm able to do what I love to do every day.

I dedicate this to my mother, Edwina Davis, who still smiles, laughs, and fights every day through life's disappointments. You are the epitome of strength and have truly made lemonade out of lemons.

Your humor is contagious, and your tough love approach has taught me to suck it up and keep it pushing, whatever "it" may be. Edwina, you are my only friend.

To my irresistible and amazing husband, Gladimir Vatel, who came into my life bringing so much love, support, and amazing Haitian food. You jumped in with both feet to support my crazy ambition without question or reservation.

My world became brighter with you in it, and there are no words to express how much I love and appreciate you. I look forward to continuing to build our life together. When I succeed, you succeed.

My Career Story

During the early days of searching for my ideal career, I didn't care about which mediocre job I got, because I knew I wasn't going to be there long. I would get something quick, putting in only minimal effort.

I'd show up late, take long lunches, text all day, and engage in far too many conversations with my coworkers. I was a social butterfly who worked every now and then.

After years of not putting forth any effort or sticking with a company long term, I realized that I had wasted years being mediocre. I'd spent years spending six months here, nine months there, with no clear direction. I had no one to tell me that I needed to get serious, focused, and strategic about my career.

I have yet to meet a career coach who will admit that they were a bad employee at one point or another. I said all of this to say, "I know how you feel!" Fortunately for you, I tried many different career strategies to find what works and what doesn't. The journey out of career schizophrenia starts with your résumé.

This guide will break down for you every skill and technique I use as a professional résumé writer to get my clients more interviews, more promotions, and ultimately more money. By the end of this process, you will be proud to tell your unique career story.

Since childhood, my focus has been on being a theater actress. I worked tirelessly in my hometown of San Francisco to eventually get to New York City, but once I arrived there at age 21, that dream slowly morphed into something completely different.

Today, I am a nationally certified résumé writer, executive career coach, author, speaker and owner of the premier résumé writing service, Career Global, based in New York City. My career advice has been published in Forbes, Yahoo Finance, Glassdoor, and Big Interview, to name a few, and I hold 3 distinguished industry-based career certifications, Certified Career Transition Coach (CCTC), Credentialed Career Manager (CCM), and is one of approximately 60 Nationally Certified Résumé Writers (NCRWs).

Document Strategy

Before we dive into the individual elements that make a résumé great, let's discuss the characteristics of great résumés in their entirety.

SALES-FOCUSED

Your résumé is the ultimate sales pitch. You are selling your benefits, not your features. What does that mean? It means that you are writing with the reader in mind, communicating the benefits you bring to their company, not what you want from a company. Consider your résumé an inverted pyramid, putting the most relevant information first.

It should include action language, focuses on your achievements, and convey an overall image of quality. For example:

Sell Your Value in <u>Your Opening Summary:</u>

Before: I am seeking a position to leverage my 12 years of sales experience where I can develop my skills further, as well as, learn new industries and practices.

After: Creative thinker well-versed in mitigating risk while simultaneously reducing cost, improving operational processes and increasing profitability.

Sell the Benefits in your <u>Job Description:</u>

Before: Manage budgets in excess of $50 million for multiple networks.

After: Presided over **$50M** budgets delivering monthly reconciliations, expense forecasts and analyses for varying networks according to GAAP standards.

RELEVANT

Why waste valuable résumé real estate with information that just doesn't matter?

Include quantifying data (where applicable), de-emphasize irrelevant information, and only includes the information that targets the position.

VISUAL WOW FACTOR

Modern résumés out rank traditional résumés any day, and this guide will focus on modern formats for that reason.

Using design elements that complement your profession is one of the best ways to ensure that you get a second look.

HIGH QUALITY

This should be self-explanatory, but it's imperative that you are meticulous in proofreading all documents and ensuring they're error free. We will discuss this further in the grammar chapter, but details include:

- ✓ Formatting, punctuation, and capitalization
- ✓ Number use (numerical or written out)
- ✓ Consistent line spacing and abbreviations

Mastering Grammar

You experience a fair amount of pressure being a professional résumé writer. People make the investment in you to get results, and documents need to be perfect, period. Would you buy a product if the advertisement had grammar and punctuation errors?

Even if you are applying for an entry-level position, there's no room for error. There are many exceptions to grammatical rules, so when in doubt never assume you're right.

Check the dictionary, a thesaurus, or even better The Gregg Reference Manual for confirmation. Here's an overview regarding the most used rules on a résumé:

NUMBERS

You should use figures and charts whenever possible. Hiring managers love quantifiable data like sales, profits, costs, etc. Vague adjectives such as "significant" or "outstanding" will not have the same impact.
In addition to making that impact, including numbers allows for quick comprehension. For example:

"Reduced credit balance **$1.7M** by creating and spearheading projects designed to initiate new collection strategies."

If you don't have stellar numbers to include, it's not a deal breaker. You can still give your résumé impact by eliminating passive language. Your résumé should not be written as a to-do list. It's important to include powerful and active language as much as possible.

The *Gregg Reference Manual* states that you:

- ✓ Spell out numbers one through 10.
- ✓ Use figures for numbers above 10.

When using a number as the first word in a sentence, it should always be spelled out. For example:

Right: <u>Thirty-nine</u> managers arrived at the conference this morning.
Wrong: <u>39</u> managers arrived at the conference this morning.

ABBREVIATIONS

There are two rules for using abbreviations. First, use them sparingly. Second, be consistent. Spell out the abbreviation the first time it is used (unless very well known in your industry) with the abbreviation in parentheses. If used again within the document, the abbreviation can be used instead of its full spelling. For example:

Option One: "The American Kidney Fund (AKF)." This is best for readers who are not familiar with the foundation.

Option Two: "HVAC." If you're in the heating and cooling industry, you know that stands for "Heating, Ventilation, and Air Conditioning."

Don't use periods in abbreviations.

HYPHENATION

Hyphenation is complicated and varies according to style. Be sure to familiarize yourself with the basic rules. One of the most common mistakes with hyphens is hyphenating adverbs. (It's "finely tuned" not "finely-tuned.")

REDUNDANCY

Don't use the same word twice in a single sentence or paragraph. Keep an eye out for repetitive, bloated structures and clichés like:

- "And also"
- "As to whether"
- "Due to the fact"
- "Each and every"
- "Point in time"
- "Time period"
- "In order to"
- "Considered to be"

CAPITALIZATION

This can be the trickiest rule of all and for some it's obvious to see what needs to be capitalized in résumés, cover letters, and basic writing you learned in school.

A refresher of what to capitalize wouldn't hurt, right? Here's a quick rundown:

- ✓ Capitalize the first word in a sentence, first word in a bullet point, proper nouns, name of universities or colleges, specific departments, days of the week and month – NOT seasons, names of locations (cities, states, countries}, languages, titles of jobs you've held, brand names.

Do capitalize a title if used as a résumé heading or if it <u>precedes</u> of a name.

- ✓ Director of Communications
  (2002–Present)

- ✓ VP of Communications Natalie Smith

Do not capitalize a title if it <u>follows</u> a name.

- ✓ Natalie Smith, director of homeland security.

Do not capitalize a job title if writing text or summaries.

- ✓ As director of sales, drove increase in revenue 10% within first three months.

This can be the trickiest rule of all. For many of us, it's not obvious what needs to be capitalized in résumés and cover letters, so a refresher on capitalization can't hurt, right? Here's a quick rundown:

- ✓ Capitalize the first word in a sentence, the first word in a bullet point, proper nouns, names of universities or colleges, specific departments, days of the week and months (NOT seasons), names of locations, languages, and brand names.

Do capitalize a title when used as a résumé heading, or if it <u>precedes</u> a name.

- ✓ Director of Communications
  (2012–Present)

- ✓ VP of Communications Natalie Smith

Do not capitalize a title if it <u>follows</u> a name.

- ✓ Natalie Smith, director of homeland security.

Do not capitalize a job title in text or summaries.

- ✓ As director of sales, drove increase in revenue 10% within first three months.

Résumé Styles

While résumé formats come and go, there are still four main groups, depending on what type of career history you have. Here's an overview.

REVERSE CHRONOLOGICAL

This is the most used and most preferred look. This type of format starts with your most current job and works its way backwards to your older positions.

It's the #1 choice of recruiters and hiring managers, because it makes it easy to scan the most important information and quickly rule out whether or not you're the right candidate.

There's no way to get around the fact that hiring managers are interested in your most recent work. If your most recent work is impressive and related to the position you're applying for, this is definitely the way to go. Overall, this is the format of choice.

FUNCTIONAL

This résumé format puts your skills at the forefront and leaves your actual employment details, such as responsibilities and dates, for later.

In this type of résumé, you list the skill and follow it with achievements that prove you have that skill. Your previous employers are represented by company name, location, and dates of employment.

Candidates with many gaps in employment history or who are career changers may favor this style. But be careful when choosing the functional résumé format, since some employers dislike it.

TARGETED

Typically, a targeted or combination résumé will feature a summary, qualifications, and a functional skills section.

This is followed by a reverse chronological list of jobs including only company names, locations, and dates of employment—much like the functional résumé format described above.

A targeted résumé works best when targeting a specific position and trying to showcase your most relevant qualifications.

CURRICULUM VITAE

A curriculum vitae (Latin for "the course of one's life"), also known as a CV, is used primarily to emphasize your educational credentials in the academic, medical, or scientific realms.

All CVs begin with your highest level of education and list everything you've done professionally, including publications, projects, presentations, honors, academic projects, and grants.

You will not go with a modern look here. CVs are traditional in appearance and conservatively written. Most CVs span multiple pages.

Design, Style, and Typeface

With an average of 250 applicants per corporate job opening, the last thing you want to do is to blend in with all the other plain pieces of paper. Don't be afraid of color and design.

Classic design elements such as borders, colored headers, watermarks, and other distinguishing features will enhance your résumé content.

Companies spend millions on strategically placed advertising in order to attract our attention and get us to buy things. More often than not, we buy because we like the story the company told. Your résumé should tell a story.

Design of your résumé begins with your name as your header. Consider designing a consistent look and feel for your name and address that carries through all of your cover letters and reference pages.

Don't get me wrong, you don't want your résumé looking like a bag of Skittles candy. Unless you're in a creative field like graphic design, fashion, or music, stay conservative with your color choices.

No matter what color you decide to use, keep it consistent. If you're having trouble deciding, you can't go wrong with shades of blue!

Whatever design or style elements you decide to use, being consistent throughout is critical. Don't forget:

- ✓ Spacing around sections
- ✓ Line and bullet spacing
- ✓ Bullet size
- ✓ Text alignment
- ✓ Indentations
- ✓ Bolding

Less is more. There's no need for overkill. Include round bullets, check marks, boxes, dashes, and wingdings, but don't overdo it. A fussy looking résumé is not impressive and makes you look like you're trying too hard.

WHITE SPACE

What is white space, anyway? It's the space around the text. I describe white space as résumé real estate. Using appropriate white space guides the reader's eye towards important information such as bulleted lists and titles.

XYZ Medical; Philadelphia, PA
Lead Hospice Biller | 2010–2015

DASHES VS. HYPHENS

There are three distinct types of dashes:

✓ **Hyphen:** Used to join two words (i.e., full-time).

✓ **En Dash:** This is a medium-sized dash (the size of the letter "N") that is used for ranges, like between dates (i.e., 2012–2014).

✓ **Em Dash:** This is a longer dash (the size of an "M") used to indicate a parenthetical or break in thought. (i.e. Worked with Fortune 500 clients—including AT&T and Verizon—on strategic planning.)

AMPERSANDS

There are only a few situations where ampersands (&) are necessary in résumé writing, and they should only be used in those exceptional cases.

✓ **Categories:** Education & Certifications

✓ **Company Names:** Klein & Co.

✓ **Well-Known Industry Terms:** P&L

HYPERLINKS

Having your e-mail address, website, and LinkedIn profile as active links on your résumé works if it will be viewed in Microsoft Word, Adobe PDF, or other similar applications. For an ASCII or ATS-optimized version, there shouldn't be any live links.

FONTS AND SIZES

It's important to stick to a font size that's easy to read, usually 10 to 12 for the body of a résumé. Headers should be larger to draw the reader's eye.

To ensure your formatting doesn't change every time you open the file on a different computer, keep your résumé fonts universal and clean. Some of the best fonts include Book Antiqua, Arial, Tahoma, Verdana, Calibri, and Cambria.

Stay away from Times New Roman! It's overused and seen as dull in the industry.

Gathering Information

Your résumé isn't just a list of job duties and dates. You need to provide context and color that demonstrate your value.

START WITH THE BASICS

You may be thinking, *"Of course I have company name and employment dates...."* I want you to think beyond that. For some of you, this is the easiest part of the process, because you can just base it on your old résumé. I'm going to ask you to go a bit deeper.

Yes, you need basic information like dates of employment, positions held, etc., but you also need to include things you might not have thought about. It will help you in this process to learn more about the company you work or worked for.

Research the company's size, annual profit, mission statement, company vision/mission statement, and descriptions. Most of this information will be located on the company website.

In addition, gather any recommendations, performance reviews, or even glowing emails you've received. All of those things count!

Don't just think of mundane things you did in each position. You answered the phone, filed papers, set up meetings.... Boring!

Your descriptions should not be boring. Think about the results you've achieved, not what you've done. It's important to think through a complete story, with a beginning, a middle, and an end.

Here is an example of the thought process you should have when listing your achievements.

Company Name: Nelson's Bagel Company
Top Cleveland-based company shipping across 15 states, with annual revenue of $18 M.
Location: Cleveland, OH 44103 **Dates:** 2013 to 2016
Position: Corporate Strategy Associate

What have I accomplished? Did I work on any projects? What was my role? Explain the stages of the project you worked on and include the results.

What was accomplished as the result of my involvement? Hiring managers love numbers that paint a picture of what you can do and the results are measurable. For example:

Before: *Answered phones.*

After: *Answered 6-line telephone averaging 80 inbound and outbound calls per day.*

Just by adding a few numbers, the description comes to life and paints a picture of the volume you can handle. See the difference?

If it's not possible to add measurable results, that's not a deal breaker, however, you need to tell the whole story of the problem you were hired to solve, what you implemented to solve that problem, and the results of your involvement.

Numbers shouldn't be thrown in just because. Be prepared to explain how the results were achieved in an interview. If you're unable to do that, it's best to just leave out.

Building a résumé foundation isn't always fun, but it's necessary to ensure your document is as great as it needs to be.

Building Your Résumé

Now that you have a grasp of everything you need, let's begin putting it into action.

HEADER

As suggested earlier, it's best to design a unique letterhead that makes a memorable opening statement. It doesn't take much to do this in Microsoft Word.

1. Open a blank page.
2. Set new page margins by clicking the **Page Layout** tab.
3. Click the **Margins** option dropdown menu and choose the suggested **Narrow** margin option, which will create 0.5" margins on all sides.

I like the narrow margin because it allows you to maximize the page. For example, this résumé letterhead is easy to design:

> Business Development | Talent Acquisition | Process Improvement | Project Management
> **HEATHER ANDERSON**   Eaton, CO 80615 | 970.402.2242 | heathera@myemail.com

Once you choose your font color and alignment, click the **Shading** icon in your Microsoft Word header to play with the colors and see what works for you.

This header has design elements beyond the traditional style, yet it's not too busy and has industry-specific keywords front and center.

To see the difference, here's a typical traditional header, in Times New Roman, which lacks that WOW factor you need. There's nothing memorable about this header, and it doesn't take advantage of a branding opportunity.

> **HEATHER ANDERSON**
> 123 Main Street, Eaton, CO 80615 – (970) 402-2242
> heathera@myemail.com

Before you get to the opening value summary, you need to communicate to the reader your position and brand promise. For example:

SENIOR CORPORATE BUSINESS STRATEGIST
Discovering innovative ways to close foundational business loopholes and drive bottom-line results.

There's no confusion about <u>who you are</u>, <u>what you offer</u>, and <u>what position you're applying for</u>. The reader can visualize you filling a gap in their company structure. It's wise to play with the title for each submission in order to ensure you present yourself as a great fit.

If you have your eye on a business development executive, corporate strategy associate, or operations manager position, the above can easily be adjusted to satisfy each of these opportunities.

Your résumé should be written in a way that avoids the need for constant updating and changes to content. Draft your résumé so that changing the title is enough. The last thing you want is for a recruiter and hiring manager to pick up your résumé and have no idea what you do.

SUMMARY

Your opening summary (a.k.a. career summary or professional profile) is like the trailer to a blockbuster movie. Movie studios invest money in trailers to whet our appetites for the full movie and get us to buy tickets.

Your summary is a preview of the entire résumé and needs to entice the hiring manager to keep reading. It has to show them why you're the one they need to hire.

Your summary answers their most important question: "What can you do for us?" Remember, it's not about you and your needs.

Many years ago, you could start with an objective listing what you needed. You could talk about what you wanted from a company or your career. Sound familiar?

These days, the first step to creating an impressive sales pitch is understanding the characteristics and skills you're bringing to the table.

Can you save the company money? Make them money? Improve their customer service? Overhaul their operational strategy? Once you understand those points, you'll be able to explain how you can give them what they want.

If there's a specific position you're interested in, this would be the place where you would begin to utilize the job description. Use the job description as a guide only for presenting your most relevant and important skills and experience.

Instead of building your résumé from the perspective of your experience, begin by understanding the key requirements in the job description and highlight how your qualifications meet their requirements. For example:

Business Development Manager Job Description:

*Our next **customer-focused** business development manager must possess the **analytical ability** to generate **profitable business growth**, have strong **account management** skills, and **cultivate business partnerships.***

Based on the job description, here's a summary opening that makes sense.

Forward-thinking and highly adaptable business development strategist who innovates process solutions that generate long-term business growth. Transforms struggling businesses by deploying strategies aimed at exceeding fiscal benchmarks by developing business partnerships and customer-focused systems.

Your summary shows how you can solve the employer's problems. It shouldn't be more than 4–5 lines.

Continue to build your value proposition and separate yourself from the crowd by adding a combination of technical skills, professional credentials, and education or training if you're a new graduate.

Tips:

- ✓ **Do not** overemphasize overused, generic, transferable skills, since everyone has them.

- ✓ **Do** use a thesaurus. There are many ways to say "develop" or "create." Don't be redundant.

- ✓ **Do** make sure you back up the claims made in your summary with accomplishments that prove the statement in the Career Experience section.

- ✓ **Do** include as many facts as possible. Think impressive career highlights that you can prove within your professional history.

KEYWORD-DENSE SKILLS

When it comes to Applicant Tracking Systems (ATS), keywords are of extreme importance. It's impossible for your résumé to be complete without industry-specific keywords. They are the glue that holds all the pieces together.

I'm not referring to general keywords like "team player," "oral communication skills," etc. Remember, you're selling your benefits as a candidate.

If you choose to include a key skills section, make sure you include a minimum of 9 entries.

How to find the best ones? The answer lies in your industry and position.

What skills are most important to making someone successful in the position you want? Once you've brainstormed, narrow them down. Remember, you also have the option of not including a key skills section at all.

These days, it's getting more common to eliminate the key skills section and expand the skills within the résumé. Either way is acceptable.

PROFESSIONAL EXPERIENCE

Now that you've gotten your hiring manager to keep reading, it's time to back up your claims. Your job descriptions should start out strong and sustain the reader's interest by emphasizing the key skills mentioned earlier.

One of the worst things you can do is include, "responsible for" or "duties include." By using keywords and action verbs instead, you will energize your job description and continue to keep the reader's attention.

Hiring managers want to hire candidates who can make an immediate impact and go above and beyond the call of duty.

Always start with active verbs. Whether a reader is viewing your résumé for 5 seconds or 5 minutes, starting sentences with action verbs allows you to best communicate your achievements.

Your job description should flow and include promotions, projects, special assignments, awards. and, of course, quantifiable achievements.

Keep in mind that the word "by" is unnecessary and redundant in résumé speak. It's best to state that you, "increase revenue 10%" not "increase revenue _by_ 10%."

Need help with the numbers? Try developing these number-oriented achievements by comparing your performance to a goal or to an industry average.

If you don't have the numbers, you can still make your job descriptions dynamic by implementing the 3-part method explained above. Show how you made an impact by including what you did, how you did it, and the result.

Also, make sure current jobs are written in present tense and previous jobs in past tense.

Before: Negotiated and won new accounts with high-end clientele.

After: Delivered **$10M** in sales over 15 years, negotiating and winning new accounts with high-end clientele.

DATES

Employment dates are probably the last thing you want to think about, but they're a detail you shouldn't overlook.

If you decide to add employment dates in the typical spot on the far right margin, keep in mind that if you have short-term employment, having it in this position will draw more attention.

To help de-emphasize a short term of employment, use years only, not months. Instead of "November 2015 to February 2016" or "11/15 to 2/16," simply state "2015 to 2016." You can go into more detail in the interview.

JOB DESCRIPTION

Before you begin listing bulleted achievements, you need to prepare the reader for those achievements.

You do this by offering a descriptive paragraph in which you give an overview of your position. This description should not be longer than five lines in length.

If you decide to extend it longer than five lines, break the paragraph up into two or more smaller paragraphs and use categories to ensure easy reading i.e., "operational functions" in one paragraph and "sales functions" in the next.

When readers see very long paragraphs, their eyes can glaze over and they could lose interest in reading further.

BULLETS

When you list your achievements, stick to a maximum of five bullets. If you include more than five, consider using keywords to differentiate. If you're adding more information, then make it worth it. For example:

- ✓ **BUSINESS ACUMEN:** Decreased mileage costs $360K over 2016 by applying sourcing strategy to maximize existing load capacity and reduce incremental mileage between distribution hubs.

- ✓ **COST REDUCTION:** Reduced equipment carrier budget $2M by creating companywide procedures for equipping facilities to accurately handle equipment input and output.

With this technique, you have the option of avoiding a separate key skills section. Comparing the two options will tie everything together.

Traditional Career History Layout:

XYZ Medical, Philadelphia, PA
May, 2010 – July, 2015
Lead Hospice Biller
- Audited patient medication records. Solely responsible for updating patient information based on nurse and doctor requests regarding the medication therapy of each patient.
- Interacted extensively with facilities, hospitals, and third-party vendors to assess a patient's needs.
- Instrumental in building hospice department policies and billing procedures.
- Wrote literature for hospice billing.
- Consistently passed audits with a 98% rating.

What's wrong here? While this format gets right to the point, it fails to impress and reads like a to-do list. To paint a complete career story, you must follow what I call a three-part method.

For example, the client has consistently passed audits with a 98% score, but there's no information as to **how** this was achieved. Hiring managers want to know how you will achieve the same thing for them. Take note of this revamped example:

Modern Career History Layout:

XYZ Medical; Philadelphia, PA
Lead Hospice Biller | 2010 – 2015

Oversaw 5-member billing team handing day-to-day medical billing operations for third party clients and vendors. Partnered with top medical clinics, hospitals, and third-party vendors to properly assess patient care and update patient portfolios with accurate medication history.

Key Accomplishments:

- ✓ Consistently received 98% medical audit scores by conducting monthly practice audits to ensure team was well versed in audit and compliance requirements.

- ✓ Increased operations accuracy 15% by developing standard operating procedures (SOPs) for 22-member billing department, methods later adopted as the "gold standard" companywide.

- ✓ Created medical billing training guide designed to enhance new hire onboarding and employee training, guaranteeing adherence to company standards.

EDUCATION

If you are a new graduate, most of your experience will be academic. If this is the case, your Education section should be placed further up, after Key Skills.

Include academic accomplishments such as majors, minors, selected coursework, internships, awards, and GPA. If your GPA is less than 3.0, do not include it.

In contrast, seasoned professionals place their education at the very end.

For those with an impressive education background, such as possessing an MBA or graduating from an Ivy League institution, this detail can be mentioned in the summary—i.e. "Harvard-educated business innovator."

Your degree can be spelled out or abbreviated. If you choose to abbreviate, each letter should be followed by a period (B.B.A., B.S., B.A., A.A., Ph.D., etc.) with no spaces.

Sample format:

B.B.A., Economics, University, City, State, Date
If you decided to write it out, it would look like this:

Bachelor of Business Administration, Economics, University, City, State, Date

Remember, if you're writing about your education in cover letter text, you do not capitalize the area of study or the degree—i.e., "As a recent college graduate from New York University with a bachelor of art in theater arts...."

Other variations include:

Bachelor of Science, Psychology
Date
Minor, Sociology
University, City, State

B.B.A., International Business, with emphasis in Finance, University, City, State, Date

Bachelor of Science in Marketing, University, City, State, Date. Dual Major: advertising and creative design

HARVARD LAW SCHOOL, City, State
Juris Doctor, Date

Master of Business Administration, Expected Date
University, City, State

Satellite Campus, Date
University of Oklahoma, Oklahoma City, OK

Biology Courses Completed, University of South Florida, City, State, Date Attended

If you graduated more than ten years ago, avoid adding graduation dates. Showing a graduation date of 1986 might make you vulnerable to age discrimination.

CERTIFICATIONS

If you have been involved in continuing education, and this training is relevant to your job target, it should be included along with other certifications and licenses in the education section. Make sure to spell out any certifications that aren't well known.

COMMUNITY INVOLVEMENT, HOBBIES, AND INTERESTS

In most cases, hobbies and interests should be eliminated. However, there are a few situations in which they are relevant. They should be included if:

- ✓ They support the employer's requirements, such as in the case of a school volunteer applying for a daycare position.

- ✓ It's directly related to the employer's qualifications, as when an amateur graphic designer applies for a job as a professional-level graphic designer.

- ✓ It shows your character, as in when you're a Big Brother/Big Sister Program volunteer applying for counselor position.

REFERENCES

If you have the proverbial "References provided on request" on your résumé, remove it. It is no longer needed to bring closure to the document.

The ATS-Friendly Résumé

Applicant Tracking Systems (ATS) is a type of software program used by companies and recruiters to save time when sifting through thousands of résumés.

When you submit your résumé, it is scanned according to the employer's criteria and scored. When hiring managers or recruiters search for keywords associated with a particular job, only the résumés with the necessary keywords or score will be seen.

Hiring managers can search for skills, experience, qualifications—pretty much anything that will allow them to find the best of the best out of thousands of candidates.

The misconception is that ATS software is still just as archaic as when it started, and that the only way to get noticed is to keep your résumé as simple and bland as possible, free from design, color, and formatting. This couldn't be further from the truth.

You don't know what kind of system your hiring manager is going to be using, so it's best to combine all the best elements of design, formatting, and content. Don't be afraid to embrace modern formats. Taking these tips into consideration when writing your résumé will ensure you maximize your chances of success getting through ATS programs. Today…

- ✓ ATS reads the code behind the formatting. Everything is done electronically.

- ✓ You can use italics, bolding, underlining, highlights, and other additions with confidence. Font colors, types, and styles no longer matter. Also, shading is okay.

- ✓ Even though fancy bullets may convert to junk characters, they have no impact on ATS compatibility and overall scoring of résumés.

- ✓ The ATS skips over graphics without impacting scoring. Graphics are invisible. You can freely use charts and graphs, smart art, monograms, text boxes, and any other visual elements you like to give your résumé that WOW factor.

- ✓ Avoid adding columns and tables to format your entire résumé. Remember to submit **.doc,** not **.docx,** formats.

Cover Letters: Brief and Bold

You should never send out a résumé without a cover letter or brief e-note. They make all the difference in your job search. It sets the stage for the rest of your candidacy review. If it doesn't grab the reader's attention from the first second, it doesn't matter whether you have the world's best résumé, because no one will ever see it.

Your cover letter should hit all the important points an employer is looking for, such as industry knowledge, technical skills, personal attributes, and experience. Keep your cover letter to approximately 250 to 300 words or less. You don't want to create an extensive essay full of ramblings before your résumé is even seen. Take a "get in and get out" approach.

Be assertive. When selling your skills, it's not a time to be modest. This is the time to shine light on your relevant accomplishments and proven performance. For your letter to be effective, you must make it a 4-point power statement.

PARAGRAPH ONE

Work to evoke emotion in the opening paragraph. Open with a question, a statement of truth, a personal experience, or simply something to make the reader laugh or cry. Address the employer's need, and present yourself as the solution, showing your biggest impact to date.

PARAGRAPH TWO

Add one to three proof points to back up your claims of being a solution. Include key accomplishments that are numbers driven and relevant. You can refer to your achievements of course, however, simply reword them to give a fresh approach.

PARAGRAPH THREE

Include a call to action that's bold, polite, and assertive. Thank the reader for their consideration and state your desired next steps of an interview or a pre-interview phone screening.

The Future of Résumés

Believe it or not résumé writing is influenced by technology. Not only are you able to incorporate more graphics and artistic choices, but you are also able to build a résumé as a PowerPoint presentation, personal website, or self-produced video you can share on social media.

With all of the creative ways you can present your expertise and build your brand, please know that these ideas only enhance your candidacy. I believe having yourname.com and a visual résumé is a great way to build your brand and expertise, however, it doesn't replace a physical résumé.

When writing this book, I wanted to share strategies and techniques that will never go out of style. As long as you keep your résumé reader focused, convey your benefits, and sell your expertise as an asset to an employer, you'll be in good shape.

Putting It All Together

(Contact Information)

TARGET POSITION
(What's your overall brand promise?)

Your summary our opening summary is your sales pitch. It's not about you, it's about the reader. Explain what you're bringing to the position. For example, can you save the company money, make them money, improve company culture, etc. Include the special abilities you're known for. Whatever your value promise is, make sure it's backed up in the rest of your résumé. It's always best to show and not tell. How do you do what you do? This should be no more than 4 – 5 lines.

_____

_____

_____

_____

_____

_____

LIST YOUR TOP INDUSTRY-RELATED KEY SKILLS

_____	_____
_____	_____
_____	_____
_____	_____
_____	_____

CAREER HIGHLIGHTS SECTION (OPTIONAL)

This is a great place to add a quote from an employer, client, or colleague. Quotes solidify your expertise and allows the hiring manager or recruiter to see you as more than a name on a page. If you can't utilize a quote or LinkedIn recommendation, you can add a quote from yourself explaining what a leader in the industry you are. This is the ONLY place you can add pronouns.

→ **Career Highlight #1**

_____

_____

_____

→ **Career Highlight #2**

_____

_____

_____

→ **Career Highlight #3**

_____

_____

_____

PROFESSIONAL EXPERIENCE (COVERS 10 TO 15 YEARS OF EXPERIENCE ON AVERAGE)

Company Name; City ST | Start Date – End Date

Here you will include a brief description of company/organization including indication of size and scope (i.e. number of employees, clients, annual profits, etc.)

Position #1

Write your **Overview Statement** here – this describes your position and what you were hired to do. This should be no more than 3 – 4 lines on average.

Key Achievements:

→ Use the bullet points to list your accomplishments– for example, the projects you managed, the new systems or processes you implemented, the number of staff you managed.

→ Include numbers and other tangible results

→ Use **Action words** (Managed, Implemented, Created) to describe what you did, and **Results-focused words** (Resulting, Ensuring, Reducing, Enabling) to describe the result.

→ List between 3 and 4 accomplishments per position (can list more depending on the length of your employment).

_____; _____ | _____ to _____

Here you will include a brief description of company/organization including indication of size and scope (i.e. number of employees, clients, annual profits, etc.)

Position: _____

Write your **Overview Statement** here – this describes your position and what you were hired to do. This should be no more than 3 – 4 lines on average.

_____

_____

_____

_____

Key Achievements:

→ Use the bullet points to list your accomplishments– for example, the projects you managed, the new systems or processes you implemented, the number of staff you managed.

_____

_____

→ Include numbers and other tangible results

_____

_____

→ Use **Action words** (Managed, Implemented, Created) to describe what you did, and **Results-focused words** (Resulting, Ensuring, Reducing, Enabling) to describe the result.

_____

_____

→ List between 3 and 4 accomplishments per position (can list more depending on the length of your employment).

_____

_____

→ List between 3 and 4 accomplishments per position (can list more depending on the length of your employment).

_____

_____

→ List between 3 and 4 accomplishments per position (can list more depending on the length of your employment).

_____

_____

KEYWORDS AND INDUSTRY TERMS TO INCLUDE (REMEMBER, JOB DESCRIPTIONS ARE ONLY A GUIDE.)

_____

_____

_____

_____

_____

_____; _____ | _____ to _____

Here you will include a brief description of company/organization including indication of size and scope (i.e. number of employees, clients, annual profits, etc.)

Position: _____

Write your **Overview Statement** here – this describes your position and what you were hired to do. This should be no more than 3 – 4 lines on average.

_____

_____

_____

_____

Key Achievements:

→ Use the bullet points to list your accomplishments– for example, the projects you managed, the new systems or processes you implemented, the number of staff you managed.

_____

_____

→ Include numbers and other tangible results

_____

_____

→ Use **Action words** (Managed, Implemented, Created) to describe what you did, and **Results-focused words** (Resulting, Ensuring, Reducing, Enabling) to describe the result.

_____

_____

→ List between 3 and 4 accomplishments per position (can list more depending on the length of your employment).

_____

_____

→ List between 3 and 4 accomplishments per position (can list more depending on the length of your employment).

_____

_____

→ List between 3 and 4 accomplishments per position (can list more depending on the length of your employment).

_____

_____

KEYWORDS AND INDUSTRY TERMS TO INCLUDE (REMEMBER, JOB DESCRIPTIONS ARE ONLY A GUIDE.)

_____

_____

_____

_____

_____

_____; _____ | _____ to _____

Here you will include a brief description of company/organization including indication of size and scope (i.e. number of employees, clients, annual profits, etc.)

Position: _____

Write your **Overview Statement** here – this describes your position and what you were hired to do. This should be no more than 3 – 4 lines on average.

_____

_____

_____

_____

Key Achievements:

→ Use the bullet points to list your accomplishments– for example, the projects you managed, the new systems or processes you implemented, the number of staff you managed.

_____

_____

→ Include numbers and other tangible results

_____

_____

→ Use **Action words** (Managed, Implemented, Created) to describe what you did, and **Results-focused words** (Resulting, Ensuring, Reducing, Enabling) to describe the result.

_____

_____

→ List between 3 and 4 accomplishments per position (can list more depending on the length of your employment).

_____

_____

→ List between 3 and 4 accomplishments per position (can list more depending on the length of your employment).

_____

_____

→ List between 3 and 4 accomplishments per position (can list more depending on the length of your employment).

_____

_____

KEYWORDS AND INDUSTRY TERMS TO INCLUDE (REMEMBER, JOB DESCRIPTIONS ARE ONLY A GUIDE.)

_____

_____

_____

_____

_____

_____; _____ | _____ to _____

Here you will include a brief description of company/organization including indication of size and scope (i.e. number of employees, clients, annual profits, etc.)

Position: _____

Write your **Overview Statement** here – this describes your position and what you were hired to do. This should be no more than 3 – 4 lines on average.

_____

_____

_____

_____

Key Achievements:

→ Use the bullet points to list your accomplishments– for example, the projects you managed, the new systems or processes you implemented, the number of staff you managed.

_____

_____

→ Include numbers and other tangible results

_____

_____

→ Use **Action words** (Managed, Implemented, Created) to describe what you did, and **Results-focused words** (Resulting, Ensuring, Reducing, Enabling) to describe the result.

_____

_____

→ List between 3 and 4 accomplishments per position (can list more depending on the length of your employment).

_____

_____

→ List between 3 and 4 accomplishments per position (can list more depending on the length of your employment).

_____

_____

→ List between 3 and 4 accomplishments per position (can list more depending on the length of your employment).

_____

_____

KEYWORDS AND INDUSTRY TERMS TO INCLUDE (REMEMBER, JOB DESCRIPTIONS ARE ONLY A GUIDE.)

_____

_____

_____

_____

_____

_____; _____ | _____ to _____

Here you will include a brief description of company/organization including indication of size and scope (i.e. number of employees, clients, annual profits, etc.)

Position: _____

Write your **Overview Statement** here – this describes your position and what you were hired to do. This should be no more than 3 – 4 lines on average.

_____
_____
_____
_____

Key Achievements:

→ Use the bullet points to list your accomplishments– for example, the projects you managed, the new systems or processes you implemented, the number of staff you managed.

_____
_____

→ Include numbers and other tangible results

_____
_____

→ Use **Action words** (Managed, Implemented, Created) to describe what you did, and **Results-focused words** (Resulting, Ensuring, Reducing, Enabling) to describe the result.

_____
_____

→ List between 3 and 4 accomplishments per position (can list more depending on the length of your employment).

_____

_____

→ List between 3 and 4 accomplishments per position (can list more depending on the length of your employment).

_____

_____

→ List between 3 and 4 accomplishments per position (can list more depending on the length of your employment).

_____

_____

KEYWORDS AND INDUSTRY TERMS TO INCLUDE (REMEMBER, JOB DESCRIPTIONS ARE ONLY A GUIDE.)

_____

_____

_____

_____

_____

EDUCATION/CERTIFICATIONS/LICENSES

Highest Degree (Bachelor or above)
University Name, City, ST | Year of Completion *(if less than 10 years)*

Next Highest Degree (Bachelor or above)
University Name, City, ST | Year of Completion *(if less than 10 years)*

If you have additional sections like affiliations, earlier career (over the 15-year average), community involvement, or technological expertise, simply copy and paste and change headers to add new sections before education. Education should be last.

→ **School #1**

_____

_____

→ **School #2**

_____

_____

→ **School #3**

_____

_____

→ **School #4**

_____

_____

Post-Résumé Brand Strategy

WHAT'S IN MY BRAND TOOLKIT? (I.E. COVER LETTER, RÉSUMÉ, BIOGRAPHY, NETWORKING RÉSUMÉ, BUSINESS CARDS, etc.)

_____
_____
_____
_____
_____

WHAT DO I NEED TO ADD TO MY BRAND TOOLKIT?

_____
_____
_____
_____
_____

WHAT ARE THE WAYS I CAN INCREASE MY BRAND FOOTPRINT AND GET THE RIGHT ATTENTION FROM THE RIGHT PEOPLE? (I.E. LINKEDIN, SOCIAL MEDIA, GUEST POSTING, EVENTS, STARTING MY OWN WEBSITE etc.)

_____
_____
_____
_____
_____

WHO DO I HAVE IN MY NETWORK TO WRITE A DETAILED TESTIMONIAL, REFERENCE, OR RECOMMENDATION?

_____

_____

_____

_____

_____

HAVE I GROWN MY NETWORK LATELY? (VIRTUALLY OR IN-PERSON)? IF NO, WHAT WEEKLY TASKS CAN I IMPLEMENT TO START STRATEGIC GROWTH?

_____

_____

_____

_____

_____

HAVE I MET ALL OF THE REQUIREMENTS FOR MY CAREER GOALS? IF NOT, WHAT DO I NEED TO DO TO ACHIEVE THEM? (I.E. ADDITIONAL TRAINING, CERTIFICATIONS, HANDS-ON EXPERIENCE THROUGH FREELANCING OR INTERNSHIPS, ETC.)

_____

_____

_____

_____

Common FAQs

I want to maximize my opportunities and apply for a variety of positions. Can't I just use a general résumé?

No. It may seem like a great idea to have a general résumé that can be used for multiple interests and industries, one that will give you more opportunities to be hired, but it actually has the opposite effect.

If you represent yourself as a Jack/Jane of all trades, to an employer, you're an expert in nothing. That's right, nothing. Your résumé should be targeted, with relevant expertise highlighted. The hiring manager should know what problems you solve.

How do I hide gaps in my employment?

There's no easy way to hide employment gaps. Gaps are gaps. But you can camouflage. One simple way is to only put years on your work history, not months and years. You don't have to add every job either.

You might choose to only add relevant experience, not a complete employment history. If you've done years of contract or freelance work, say so. You don't have to present all of your work history the same way.

Which résumé format is best for showcasing my skills?

Reverse-chronological order is the best format and the one favored by corporate recruiters and hiring managers due to its readability and simplicity.

How do I cut down the length of my résumé? There's a lot of important information I want to keep.
Cut the fat! Your résumé should be just a snapshot of your best achievements. You don't need everything on there. And if you have relevant experience from more than 15 years ago, you can simply list the job titles without descriptions.

If I have a résumé that's working, do I really need LinkedIn?

Yes. LinkedIn is a free professional resource available to global professionals to connect, build their brand identity, and apply to millions of open positions. Even if it's something you think you won't use, your profile will be seen by search engines, adding to your online brand identity. I have several clients who received six-figure job offers as a result of LinkedIn, so you never know what opportunities and connections can develop.

Can I use a testimonial or quote on my résumé?

Yes, when appropriate. I love using quotes on résumés when I can. It's best to keep them to around 1 to 2 sentences. They should be from leaders and/or partners you've worked with.

I'm a new graduate with barely any experience. How can I get employers to hire me?

Being a new graduate doesn't mean your résumé has to be bare bones. It's important to maximize your college experience, including internships, skills, memberships, and projects. You don't have to be a college overachiever to make an impact.

Take what you have and add as much detail as possible to give the reader an idea of your work ethic and what you have to offer. Also, don't be embarrassed if you have retail or food service work on your résumé. Everyone knows college jobs aren't glamourous.

I have a lot of professional work experience, but I'm still in school getting my master's degree. Should I format my résumé like a new graduate, with my education up front?

Most of the time, the answer is no. Your education shouldn't be at the forefront unless it's from a well-known top institution, and even then, you only do that when the employer specifically asks you to.

I know quantitative achievements are impressive, but I don't have any. How can I impress hiring managers without them?

Sometimes it's just not possible to quantify results, and that's okay. As long as your job descriptions tell a complete story that states the problem, describes what you did to solve it, and shows the results, your résumé will have impact.

How do I avoid getting discriminated against because of my age?

It's all about the dates. If you have positions or degrees dating back 20 years or more, remove the dates. You definitely don't want hiring managers to see that you graduated college in 1978 when they were born in 1978.

In addition, avoid adding years of experience. You may think that adding "...with 30 years of experience" is a good thing, but it only dates you. Don't forget about your email address. It's common to have an email address that includes your date of birth like nataliesmith1950@gmail.com, but it's best to just leave out.

Samples

Client information is private and all samples are not available for viewing. The following samples are provided with client identifying information edited for safety. Extended experience has been deleted to maintain a one-page format.

AMBER DAVIS
Oakland, CA 94606 ~ 510.922.1212 ~ amber.davis21@rocketmail.com

SENIOR ACCOUNTING & FINANCE PROFESSIONAL
FINANCIAL MANAGEMENT ~ PROJECT OVERSIGHT ~ REGULATORY COMPLIANCE

April 1, 2017

Brian Soriano
Manager
Sunrise Staffing
2854 McIntosh Blvd., Suite 19
Emeryville, CA 94608

Dear Mr. Soriano:

Searching for the best recruiter is just like searching for the best candidate. I recently began a job search in the San Francisco Bay Area and I have enlisted professional career help to introduce me to the best recruiters in the country. As a highly reputable recruiter in the financial market with an emphasis on accounting, you were at the top of the list.

Whether managing multimillion-dollar budgets, turning around failing audits, or weathering tough organizational transitions, I offer your clients a rare combination of skills and tools-in-action by:

- **A streamlined system** for record keeping, data collection, and tax season preparation proving that with the right framework, document referencing doesn't have to be difficult.

- **Best Practices** that ensure all accounting regulations are adhered to while always safeguarding against security breaches and errors.

- **High-level client support** with an open door policy for clients and their representation that allows immediate remedy of their issues.

I attached a copy of my résumé for your reference. I welcome the opportunity to speak with you and discuss how my knowledge and skills could contribute to the success of your clients. I will follow-up with you within a week to confirm receipt of this package, and to determine what next steps should be taken. I sincerely appreciate your consideration and look forward to speaking with you in the near future.

Sincerely,

Amber Davis

Enclosure: Résumé

CHRISTOPHER MUNGIN

718.222.3212
CMUNGIN@YAHOO.COM
FORT LAUDERDALE, FL
WWW.LINKEDIN.COM/IN/MUNGINC

SENIOR-LEVEL FINANCIAL AID MANAGER
MULTIFACETED FINANCIAL STRATEGIST ▶ EXCEEDING FINANCIAL BENCHMARKS

February 13, 2017

Gloria Malone
HR Director
Azuza University
2750 NW 70th Avenue
Fort Lauderdale, FL 33319

Dear M. Malone:

How many times have you heard someone say, *"I just can't afford it!"* when it comes to their education? As a seasoned financial aid officer, I hear that every day and find solutions every time.

Regardless of the challenge, I am known for maintaining integrity in decision making, exceeding quota expectations, and making an impact felt by all I work with. In my last role as financial aid administrator for New York University, I was able to:

- Reduce the default cohort rate 52%
- Increase student scholarship eligibility 75%
- Add $450K in annual revenue

In me, you will not find a candidate more dedicated to higher education and student success. I look forward to meeting with you to discuss the opportunity and my qualifications in detail. Thank you for your consideration.

Sincerely,

Christopher Mungin

Enclosure: Résumé

Michael **Smith**
ACCOUNT MANAGEMENT EXECUTIVE

New York, NY 10022 | 646-555-2222 | MikeSmith@Yahoo.com

February 14, 2017

Carol Simpson
HR Manager
Academy Billing Services
7878 Park Avenue South
New York, NY 10016

Dear M. Simpson:

Working in the fast-paced fashion industry has its perks and challenges. With my longstanding career I have learned many facets of the business, especially account management. As a highly recognized name in the billing industry, Academy Billing Services is continuously striving to give their clients an edge. Due to that stellar reputation, your posting for an Account Manager via your website peaked my interest.

As a fashion designer, I've conducted client needs assessments, maintained a high-volume of portfolios, and have gone to great lengths to make sure my clients are satisfied. Through my experiences, I have honed many transferable skills that will allow me to support the mission of your organization.

The enclosed résumé represents the depth of experience that is necessary for the position. I look forward to schedule a face-to-face interview shortly. Thank you for your time and consideration, and I look forward to speaking with you soon.

Sincerely,

Michael Smith

Enclosure: Résumé

SAMANTHA GRIFFITH, HRBP

Los Angeles, CA • (310) 777 - 3222 • Sam.Griff@Gmail.com

SENIOR-LEVEL HR & RECRUITING PROFESSIONAL
OUTSIDE THE BOX THINKER ~ RECRUITING STRATEGIST

March 29, 2017

James May
HR Manager
Greater Advanced Technology
222 180th Street W
Los Angeles, CA 90011

Dear Mr. May:

When time, money, and resources aren't an issue, it's not difficult to deliver the best new hire options and navigate HR onboarding processes with ease. However, what does a leader do when one of those three things is not an option?

Throughout my career as a recruiter and advisor, I've encountered budget constraints, language and cultural barriers, and non-existent frameworks to transform departments from the ground up.

Ready to deliver immediate and long-lasting results as Greater Advanced Technology's next Human Resources Supervisor, I am confident that my significant industry career is a perfect match for your needs and am eager to explore this opportunity with you.

Sincerely interested in further exploring this opportunity, I propose we arrange a time for us to meet where we can discuss your needs and my background in detail. Until then, thank you for your consideration.

Sincerely,

Samantha Griffith, HRBP

Enclosure: Résumé

McKenzie Taylor

2632 West 34th Street, Apt.9, New York, NY 10001
Mc.Taylor@gmail.com (917) 222-0555

Public Affairs | Law

Legal advocate breaking barriers with a commitment to community empowerment

February 8, 2017

M. Mary Ann Nichols
HR Director
The Maisley Foundation
62 Broadway
New York, NY 10005

Dear M. Nichols:

Being new to the New York area, I hit the ground running to research top organizations that could utilize my unique background which includes experience in law and community service. The Maisley Foundation made that list, so your posting for a Program Director on Idealist was a no brainer.

As an attorney, I spent nights preparing briefs, developing new initiatives, and gave more oral arguments that I'd dare to count, however, I still remember the major impact of tutoring student-athletes in college. With that one opportunity, the seed for community empowerment was planted.

Through my experiences, I have honed many skills that will allow me to support the mission of your organization. Some transferable skills you may find relevant include:

- **Developed and refined environmental policies** streamlining existing frameworks 22%.
- **Collaborated with environmental specialists** to rework community programs which reduced polluted air quality 14%.
- **Won 97% of all cases** against corporate companies making environmental violations.

I look forward to meeting with you to discuss the opportunity and my qualifications in detail. Please contact me anytime. Thank you for your time and consideration.

Sincerely,

McKenzie Taylor

Enclosure: Résumé

New York, NY 10013 | 212.555.1212 | contactemail@gmail.com | www.linkedin.com/in/marklee

MARK LEE

INFORMATION TECHNOLOGY EXECUTIVE – CIO / VP / DIRECTOR

Internationally recognized leader leveraging business development expertise to inspire innovation

Cloud Strategy & Planning ▪ International IT Security & Privacy Expert ▪ Financial IT Systems Administration

Influential technology strategist, recognized for innovating system and business solutions while simultaneously increasing profits and delivering significant cost reductions. **Highly trained project director** well-versed in financial infrastructure standards, information security, and compliance audit configurations. **Sharp business analyst** who fuels unprecedented growth by providing a clear vision and roadmaps to new business models. **Solutions-driven change agent,** backed by solid credentials and multiple certifications (CISSP, MCSE, CCNA). **Natural leader** who develops teams of all sizes and motivates diverse groups to adopt new methodologies and synergize to reach targeted metrics.

Cyber Threat Prevention ▪ Business Development ▪ Systems Integration ▪ Product Strategy & Launches ▪ Negotiations
Network Stability ▪ IT Policy Creation ▪ Crisis Management ▪ P&L Authority ▪ Recruitment & Team Leadership

HIGHLIGHTS OF DISTINCT VALUE

▪ Increased customer satisfaction an estimated **33%** by spearheading development of online banking software and FATCA US Tax Reporting automation improving user capabilities and business growth objectives.

▪ Pioneered strategic vision for company's first SharePoint corporate portal cutting server space, boosting efficiency, and accelerating query resolution.

HIGH-IMPACT EXECUTIVE COMPETENCIES

Metro Trust; New York, NY
Chief Information Officer | 2007 – Present

Recruited to oversee 22-member team of IT experts, developers, and project/legal managers as they drive application solutions and lead cloud computing initiatives. Recognized for executing companywide data management system and installing virus/firewall defense systems, backup protocols, and quality assurance while controlling €$6M budget. Designed and created strategic vision for company's SharePoint corporate portal boosting efficiency and supporting central application access.

- Reduced IT total cost of ownership (TCO) **33%** globally by restructuring hardware and software acquisitions, cutting end-user expenses, and uncovering varied productivity losses.
- Slashed support costs **60%** globally by implementing central database and creating self-sufficient users through internal support and relevant systems training.
- Decreased time to resolution (TTR) **18%** by automating identification process to unearth root cause of programming issues for immediate correction, deploying system testing to ensure errors are remedied.

EDUCATION

Bachelor of Arts Degree in Management Information Systems
New York University | New York, NY

MICHAEL WOODS, MBA, PROJECT +

254-555-9999 • contactemail@gmail.com   Columbia, Georgia

SENIOR-LEVEL FINANCE DIRECTOR
VERSATILE FINANCIAL STRATEGIST, MAXIMIZING OPPORTUNITIES AND CONNECTIONS TO EXCEED FINANCIAL BENCHMARKS

Versatile and results-driven financial executive recognized for strategic planning, development and overall day-to-day management of striving financial departments. Innate ability to empower cross-functional teams boosting morale among colleagues and students to achieve common goals. Creative thinker who continually minimizes risks while simultaneously reducing costs, improving operational processes and increasing profitability. Well-versed in federal, state, and institutional financial policies and procedures.

AREAS OF EXPERTISE

- ✓ Strategic Planning & Forecasting
- ✓ Business Development
- ✓ Sales Planning & Marketing
- ✓ Financial Planning & Analysis
- ✓ Audit Processes
- ✓ Relationship Building
- ✓ Staff Training & Leadership
- ✓ Title IV Program Guidelines
- ✓ Revenue & Profit Growth
- ✓ Project Management
- ✓ Cost Savings & Controls
- ✓ Accounting Practices

EXPERIENCE & NOTABLE CONTRIBUTIONS

Johnson School of Beauty • Bedford, TX • 2013 to 2016
Dedicated to providing students with an enriched learning environment that empowers them to develop their passion for beauty
DIRECTOR OF FINANCE
Developed and implemented strategic repositioning, restructuring, program evaluation, and full operational management for department with a keen focus on raising standards of operations, risk management, advice and student service. Provided insight and corrective action when necessary during performance evaluations ensuring consistency and efficiency at all times. Remained consistency in line with annual financial plans throughout the year and Department of Education financial facts/statements policies and procedures during document submission processes.
KEY ACCOMPLISHMENTS:
- **Reduced collection account balances 66%** by implementing new collection system to reduce student balances within weeks of tenure.
- **Decreased Default Cohort Rate 63% in one quarter**, thus preventing institution from losing federal student aid eligibility under section 435(a)(2) and section 401(j) of the Higher Education Act of 1965.
- **Increased student scholarship eligibility 1500%** by striking partnerships with local community members highlighting benefits of our student programs.
- **Grew re-entry enrollment and graduation rate 60%** by devising a tracking system geared towards ensuring student external obligation were met adjusting accordingly.
- **Added $200K in annual revenue** by making Title IV and private student loan programs available to students for the first time.
- Expert in Title IV program functions coordinating team to excellence during annual reconciliations, cash flow monitoring, internal audits, and day-to-day fiscal tasks.

EDUCATION

Masters of Business Administration
Bachelor of Science in Business Administration & Finance
FORDHAM UNIVERSITY | New York, NY (online campus) | 2016, 2014

Business Development | Contract Negotiation | CA Licensed Real Estate Agent | P & L Control
Lafayette, CA 94549 | 946.300.4837 | jamessanchez@gmail.com | www.linkedin.com/in/jamescsanchez

JAMES SANCHEZ

REAL ESTATE PROJECT MANAGER

Tenacious, results-oriented real estate project manager known for sharp business acumen, sound real estate practices, and a natural ability to develop and maintain long-term client relationships. Demonstrated ability to expand company vision of success by leveraging technology and experience to enhance client relationships that generate revenue while cutting cost. Innovative team leader skilled at driving cross-functional teams to guarantee project deadlines and budgets are met.

Real Estate Compliance ▪ Strategic Planning ▪ Data Analysis ▪ Project Planning & Execution ▪ Legal Procedures
Client Relationship Management ▪ Vendor Management ▪ Property Market Trends ▪ Real Estate Operations

Technology Expertise: Microsoft Office Suite, Adobe Creative Suite, Salesforce

PROFESSIONAL EXPERIENCE

Hightower Digital – Oakland, CA .... 2015 – Present
Project Manager, Real Estate Department

Promoted to direct 6 high-profile transit shelter contracts worth $300M+ and spanning 3K units of inventory. Oversees full real estate project life cycle ensuring contracts are in compliance with California real estate laws and statutes, coordinating process with proper owners and city officials, and supervising cross-functional teams to ensure accurate project timelines.

- **Eliminated real estate budget overages $40K annually** by launching consolidation program that successfully combined 60 digital news racks in San Francisco metropolitan area, thus eradicating nonessential real estate space.
- **Sustain 90% winning claims rate** by partnering with legal counsel to steer claims process and represent company in court.
- **Improved business processes and increased efficiency of vendor partnerships worth $18.6M by overseeing 6 vendor requests for proposal (RFP) contracts** as part of vendor selection process.
- **Spearhead full P&L management of $300M in property contracts** conducting annual forecasting and expense reporting.

Digital Media Specialist .... 2011 – 2015

Produced 100+ award-winning digital and innovative media campaigns throughout San Francisco Bay Area, leveraging strong knowledge of web technology, protocols, standards and tools. Remained up to date on emerging technologies and trends to effectively prepare local sales teams via digital training sessions.

- **Called upon to step into digital media manager role** during hiring transition, coaching and mentoring colleagues as well as third-party vendors.

AMC Worldwide – Oakland, CA .... 2010 – 2011
Business Development Manager

Hired to refocus creative and cross-platform marketing strategies in order to increase brand awareness and revenue. Prepared proposals and presentations for new and existing accounts, solidifying campaign needs according to budget. Exhibited competitive sales techniques to exceed sales goals and rapidly expand company reach.

Roadster Media, Inc. – Portland, OR .... 2008 – 2009
National Account Manager

Surged monthly sales revenue for national and local accounts $100K for *Portland Monthly*, *Seattle Metropolitan*, and *Portland Spaces* magazines, garnering print and online exposure through consultative sales techniques. Garnered company's first-ever national Mercedes Benz and BMW automotive campaigns through detailed negotiations and nurturing business relationships.

EDUCATION

Bachelor of Arts Degree, Sociology, University of California, Los Angeles

Bonus

I offer various resources I want to share with you. If you haven't already, check out www.careerglobal.co and you'll discover a wealth of posts and information that will expand the knowledge learned in this book.

Also, make sure to sign up for my email list to keep you in the loop for future trainings, webinars, videos, and new books.

If you would like additional help with your career branding documents or strategy, feel free to send me an email at info@careerglobal.co.

Action Words

Accomplished	Achieved	Adapted
Administered	Advanced	Analyzed
Attained	Balanced	Brainstormed
Budgeted	Built	Calculated
Centralized	Championed	Changed
Clarified	Coached	Collaborated
Communicated	Complied	Conceptualized
Configured	Constructed	Converted
Created	Decreased	Delivered
Demonstrated	Designed	Determined
Developed	Devised	Directed
Distributed	Documented	Earned
Eliminated	Energized	Engineered
Enhanced	Ensured	Established
Evaluated	Exceeded	Excelled
Executed	Expedited	Extracted
Facilitated	Finalized	Followed-up
Forecasted	Formed	Fulfilled
Gained	Generated	Handled
Headed	Identified	Implemented
Improved	Increased	Initiated
Innovated	Installed	Instituted
Integrated	Introduced	Investigated
Landed	Launched	Lead
Maintained	Managed	Manufactured
Maximized	Monitored	Negotiated
Operated	Optimized	Ordered
Organized	Outpaced	Outsourced
Overcame	Oversaw	Partnered
Performed	Piloted	Pinpointed
Planned	Positioned	Predicted
Prepared	Presented	Prevented
Processed	Procured	Produced

Programmed	Qualified	Quantified
Rebuilt	Rectified	Redefined
Redesigned	Re-engineered	Related
Resolved	Restored	Restructured
Revitalized	Salvaged	Satisfied
Saved	Set-up	Solved
Specialized	Streamlined	Supported
Tailored	Tested	Trained
Uncovered	Unified	Upgraded
Utilized	Validated	Wrote

Traits + Skills

Accurate	Adaptable	Agile
Capable	Collaborative	Competitive edge
Communication	Confident	Conflict Resolution
Consistent	Creative	Critical thinking
Cross-functional	Culturally Conscious	Decision-making
Detail Oriented	Determination	Diligent
Directive	Dynamic	Ethical
Effective	Efficient	Enthusiastic
Facilitator	Flexible	Focused
Follow-up	Go-getter	Hardworking
Initiative	Innovative	Integrity
Intuitive	Investigative	Judgment
Leader	Mindful	Motivated
Negotiations	Objective	Organized
Prompt	Provide	Punctual
Partnering	Passionate	Persuasive
Prepared	Proactive	Problem solve(r)
Productive	Professional	Quality
Quick learner	Reliable	Resourceful
Respectable	Respectful	Responsive
Selfless	Service	Specialist
Strategic	Tactical	Task oriented
Teamwork	Technical	Timely
Transformative	Troubleshooter	Unifying
Updated	Visionary	

CAREER GLOBAL

Want to speak to me?
I'd love to hear from you!

Phone: 888.507.8247
Email: info@careerglobal.co
Website: www.careerglobal.co

New York, NY

www.ingramcontent.com/pod-product-compliance
Lightning Source LLC
Chambersburg PA
CBHW062229220526
45471CB00009B/3407